I WANT TO DRAW™
CATS & DOGS

WRITTEN AND ILLUSTRATED BY ANTHONY J. TALLARICO

Modern Publishing
A Division of Unisystems, Inc.
New York, New York 10022

Printed in the U.S.A.

BEFORE YOU BEGIN:

The materials that you'll need are --

    NUMBER 2 PENCIL
    ERASER
    DRAWING PAPER
    BLACK FELT-TIP MARKER

Start your drawing by lightly sketching.
STEP 1. Don't be afraid to erase until you are satisfied with the way your sketch looks. This is the most important step as you will draw all the others on top of this.

STEP 2. Add this step, lightly in pencil, to the first step. Don't be afraid to draw through other shapes or to erase.

STEP 3. Add lightly in pencil. Again, don't be afraid to draw through or to erase lines or shapes you are not satisfied with.

Now you are ready to complete your drawing.
STEP 4. Finish your drawing using your black felt-tip marker. Add details and black areas. Erase all pencil marks. You can keep your drawing the way it is, in black and white, or add color.

HAPPY DRAWING!

SHORTHAIR

STEP 1: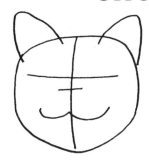

STEP 2:

STEP 3:

STEP 4:

SIAMESE

STEP 1:

STEP 2:

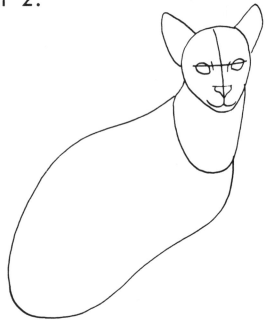

STEP 3:

STEP 4:

BURMESE

RUSSIAN BLUE

STEP 1:

STEP 2:

STEP 3:

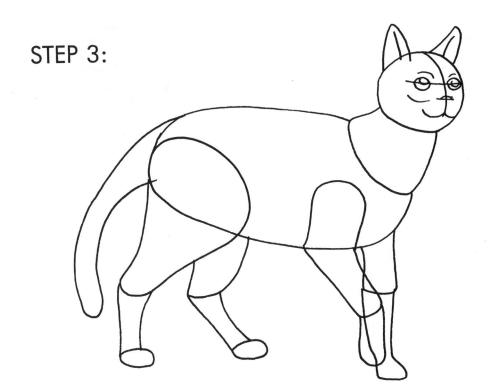

STEP 4:

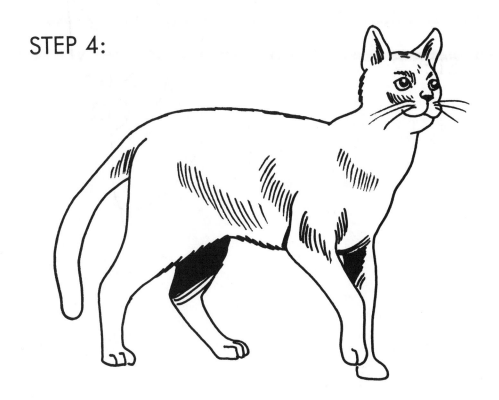

SPHYNX

STEP 1:

STEP 2:

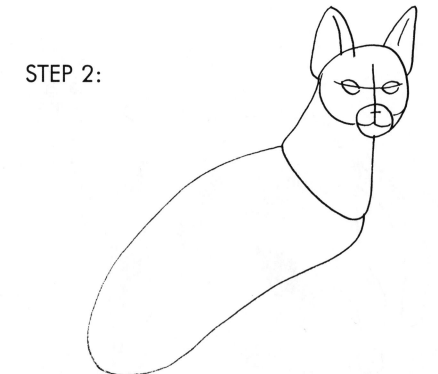

STEP 3:

STEP 4:

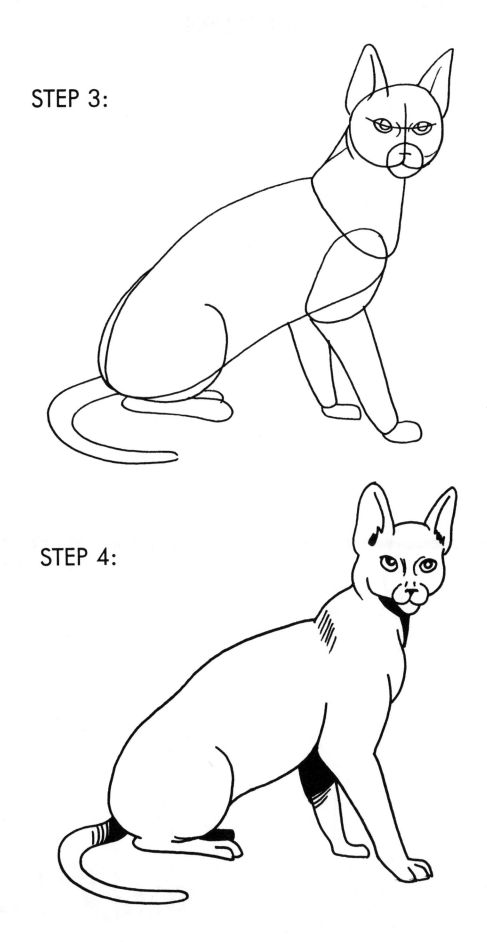

SNOWSHOE

STEP 1:

STEP 2:

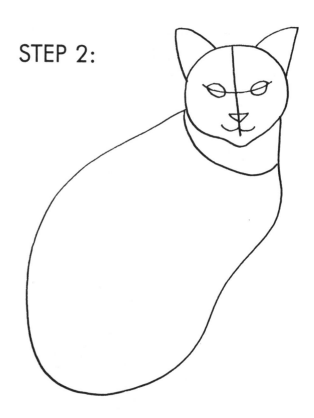

STEP 3:

STEP 4:

WIRE HAIR

STEP 1:

STEP 2:

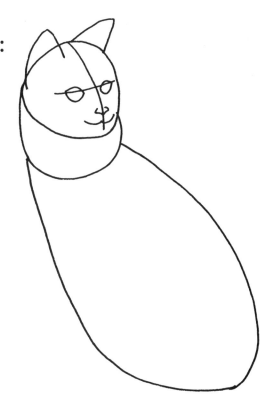

STEP 3:

STEP 4:

MAINE COON

STEP 1:

STEP 2:

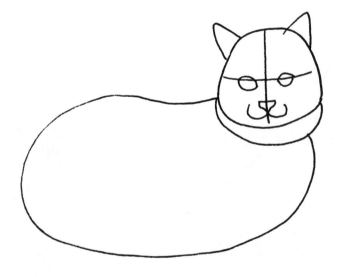

STEP 3:

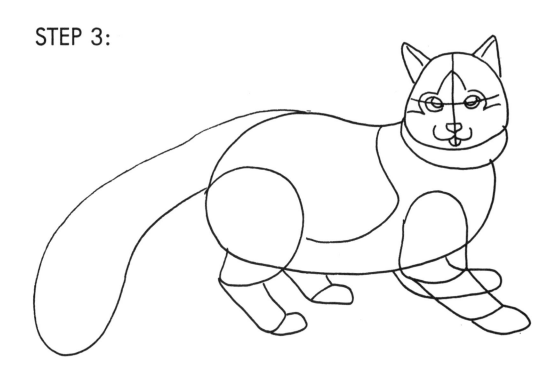

STEP 4:

BALINESE

STEP 1:

STEP 2:

STEP 3:

STEP 4:

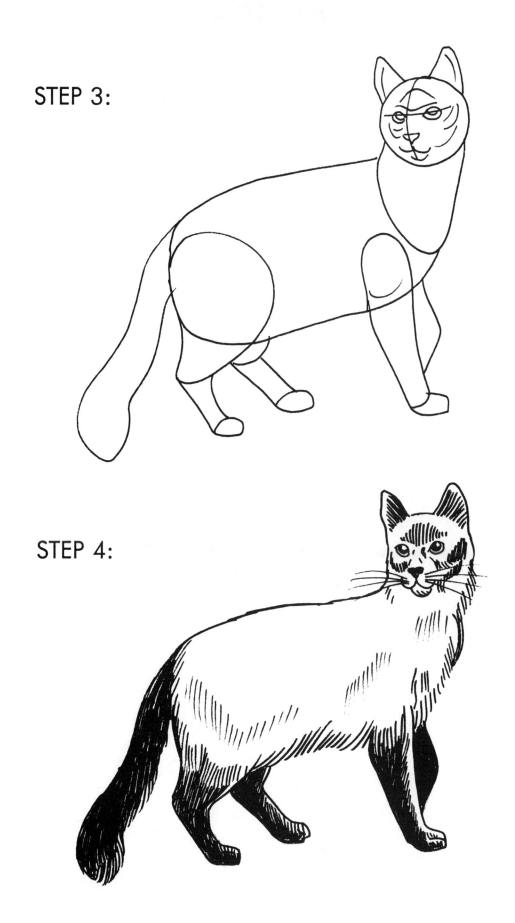

ANGORA

STEP 1:

STEP 2:

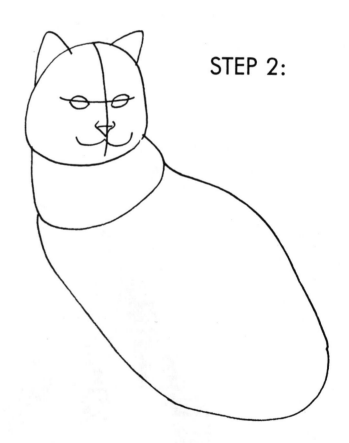

STEP 3:

STEP 4:

MANX

STEP 1:

STEP 2:

STEP 3:

STEP 4:

SINGAPURA

STEP 1:

STEP 2:

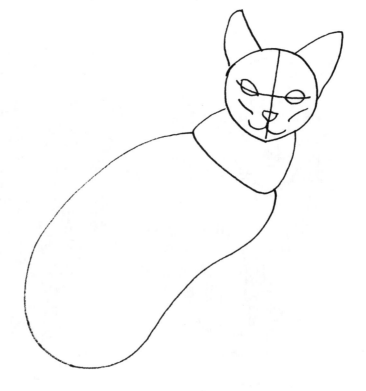

STEP 3:

STEP 4:

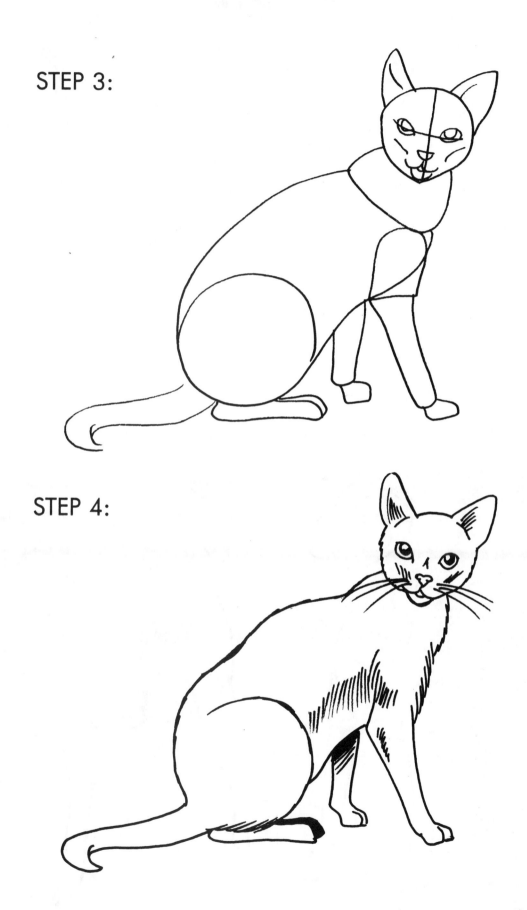

PINSCHER

STEP 1:

STEP 2:

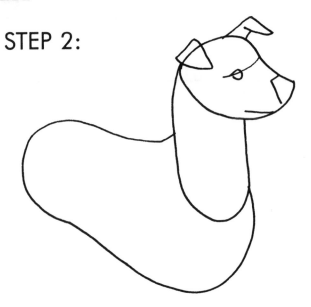

STEP 3:

STEP 4:

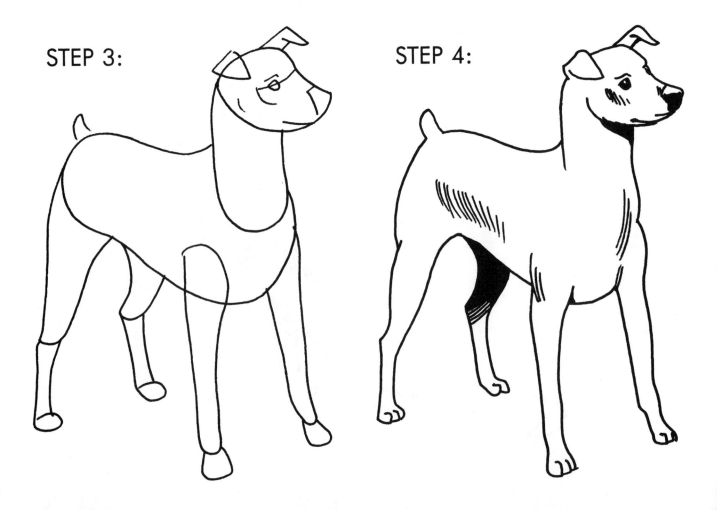

COLLIE

STEP 1:

STEP 2:

STEP 3:

STEP 4:

DALMATIAN

STEP 1:

STEP 2:

STEP 3:

STEP 4:

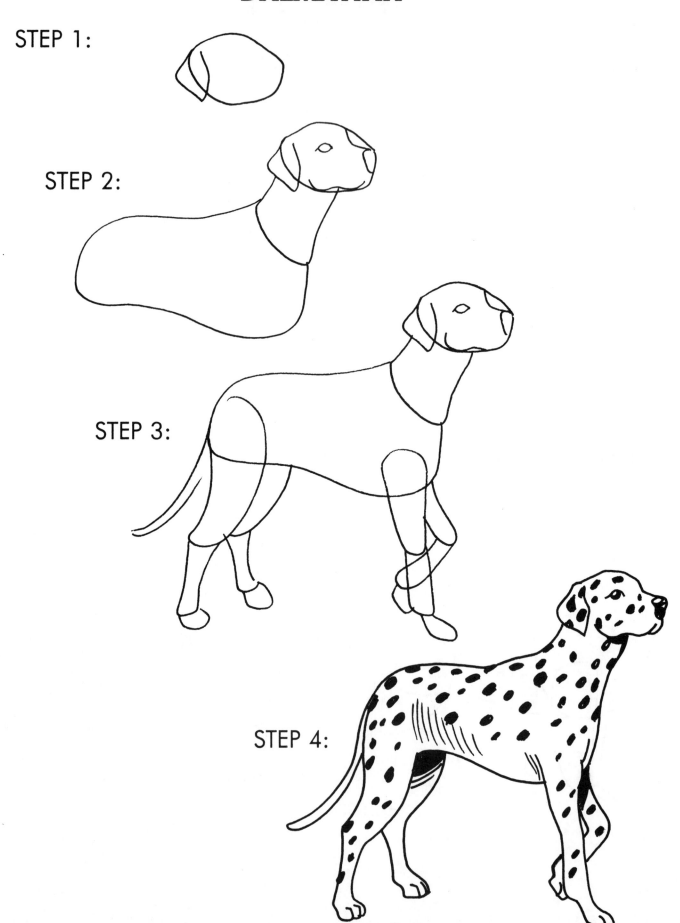

DACHSHUND

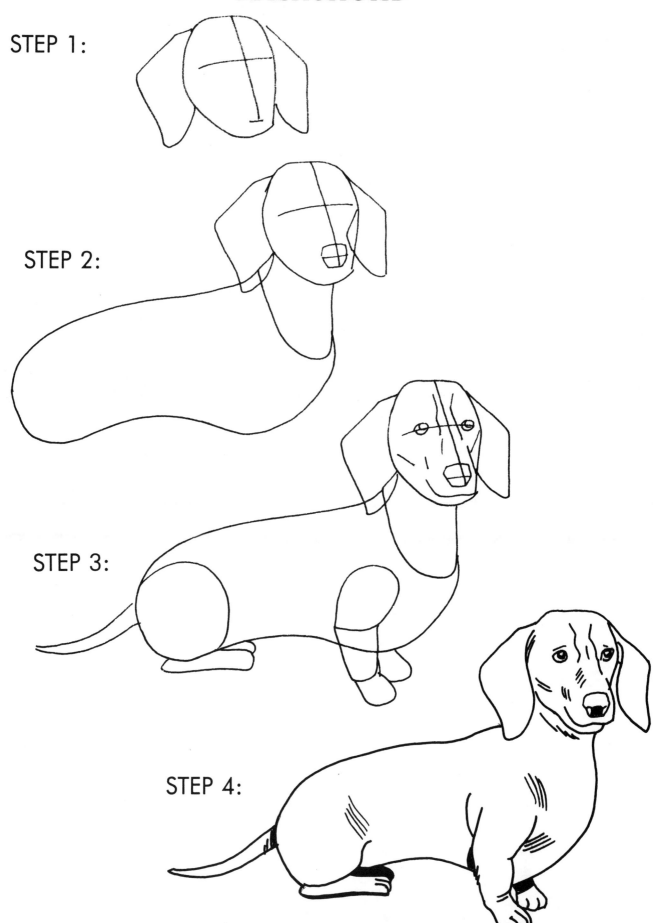

STEP 1:

STEP 2:

STEP 3:

STEP 4:

SHEEPDOG

STEP 1:

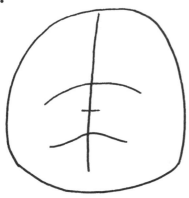

STEP 2:

STEP 3:

STEP 4:

SCHNAUZER

STEP 1:

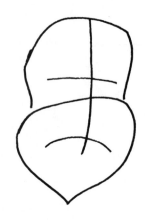

STEP 2:

STEP 3:

STEP 4:

DOBERMAN

STEP 1:

STEP 2:

STEP 3:

STEP 4:

GERMAN SHEPHERD

STEP 1:

STEP 2:

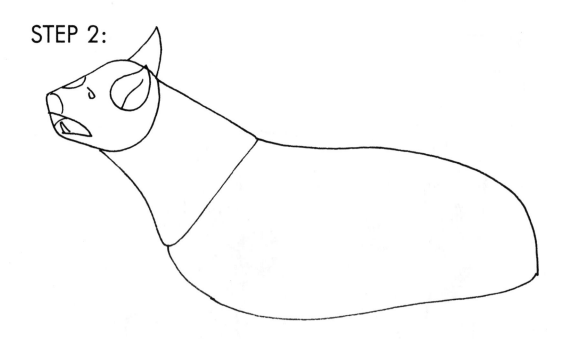

STEP 3:

STEP 4:

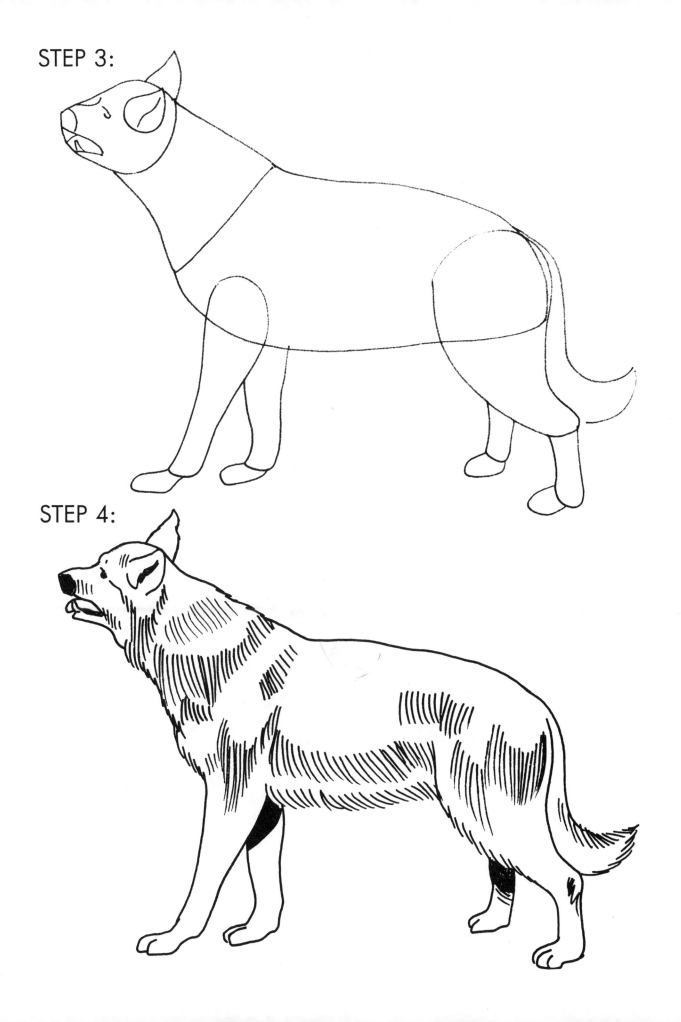

CHIHUAHUA

STEP 1:

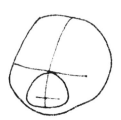

STEP 2:

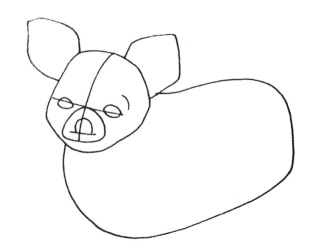

STEP 3:

STEP 4:

IRISH WOLFHOUND

STEP 1:

STEP 2:

STEP 3:

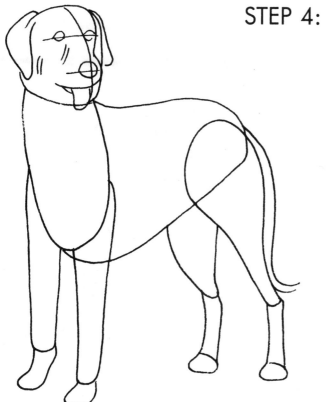

STEP 4:

SPITZ

STEP 1:

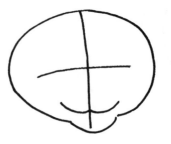

STEP 2:

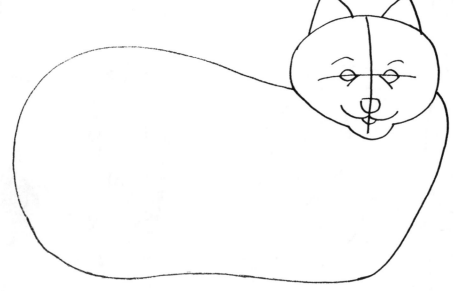

STEP 3:

STEP 4:

BEAGLE

STEP 1:

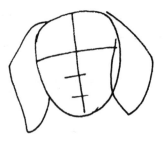

STEP 2:

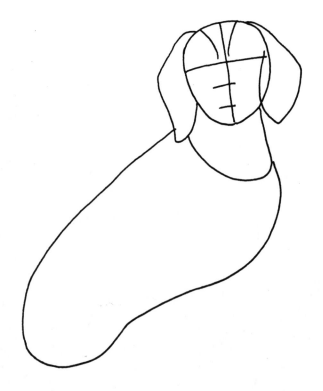

STEP 3:

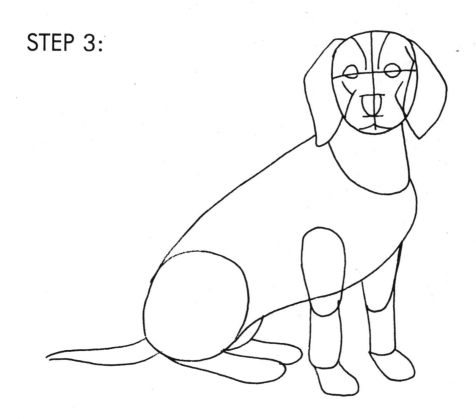

STEP 4:

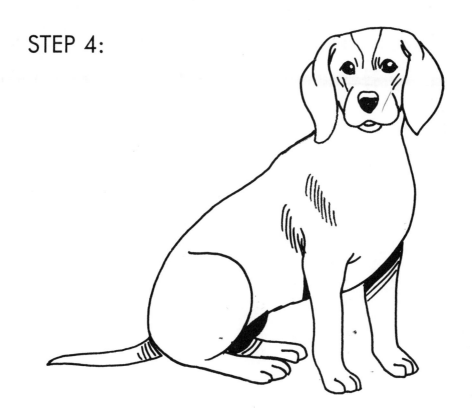

ST. BERNARD

STEP 1:

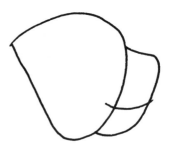

STEP 2:

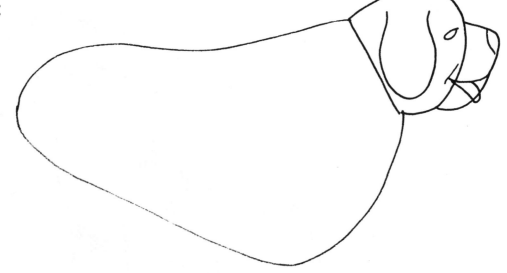

STEP 3:

STEP 4:

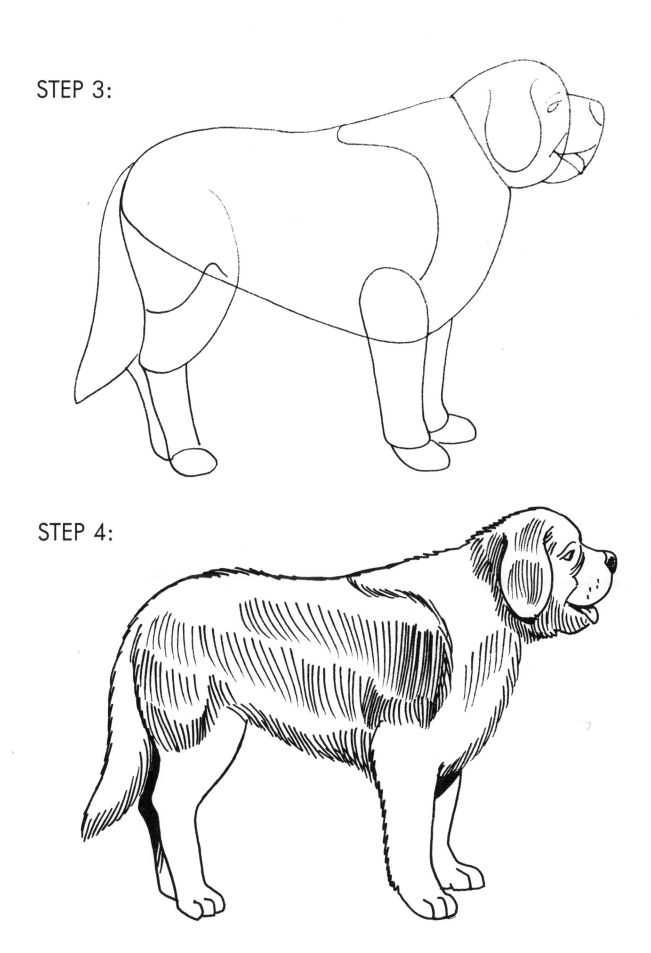

CORGI

STEP 1:

STEP 2:

STEP 3:

STEP 4:

GOLDEN RETRIEVER

STEP 1:

STEP 2:

STEP 3:

STEP 4:

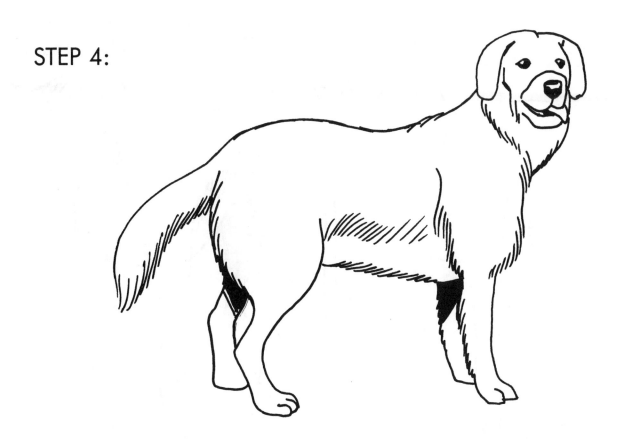

GREYHOUND

STEP 1:

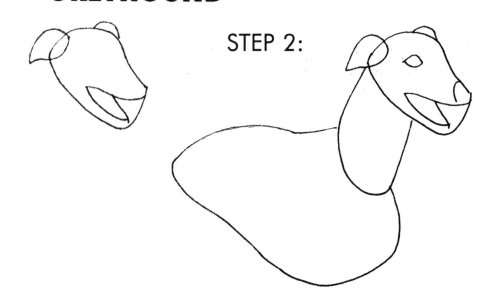

STEP 2:

STEP 3:

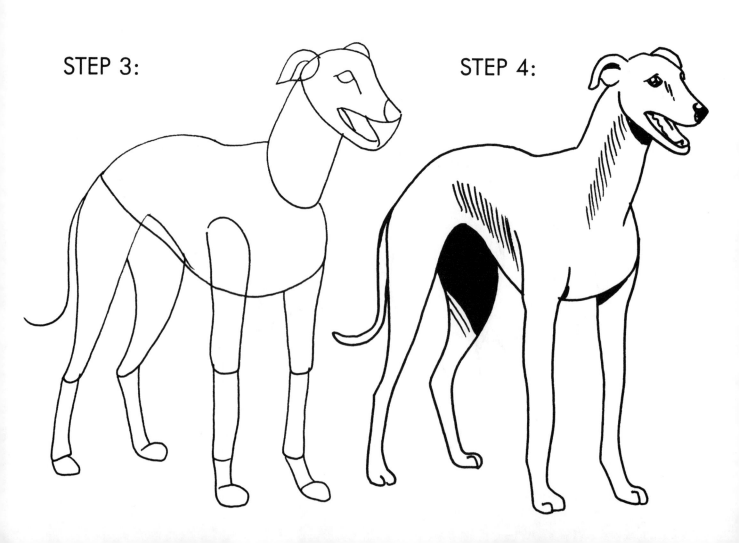

STEP 4:

CHOW CHOW

STEP 1:

STEP 2:

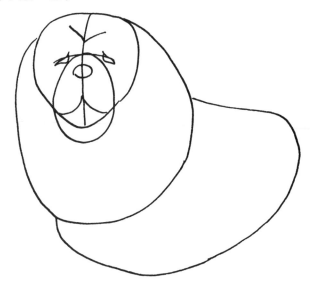

STEP 3:

STEP 4:

POODLE

STEP 1:

STEP 2:

STEP 3:

STEP 4:

LABRADOR RETRIEVER

STEP 1:

STEP 2:

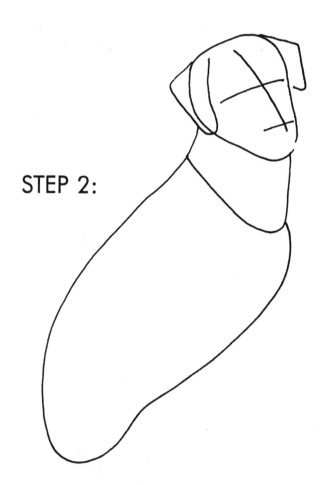

STEP 3:

STEP 4:

AIREDALE

STEP 1:

STEP 2:

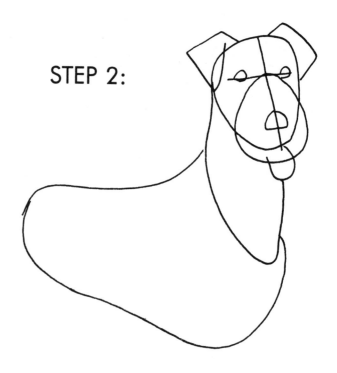

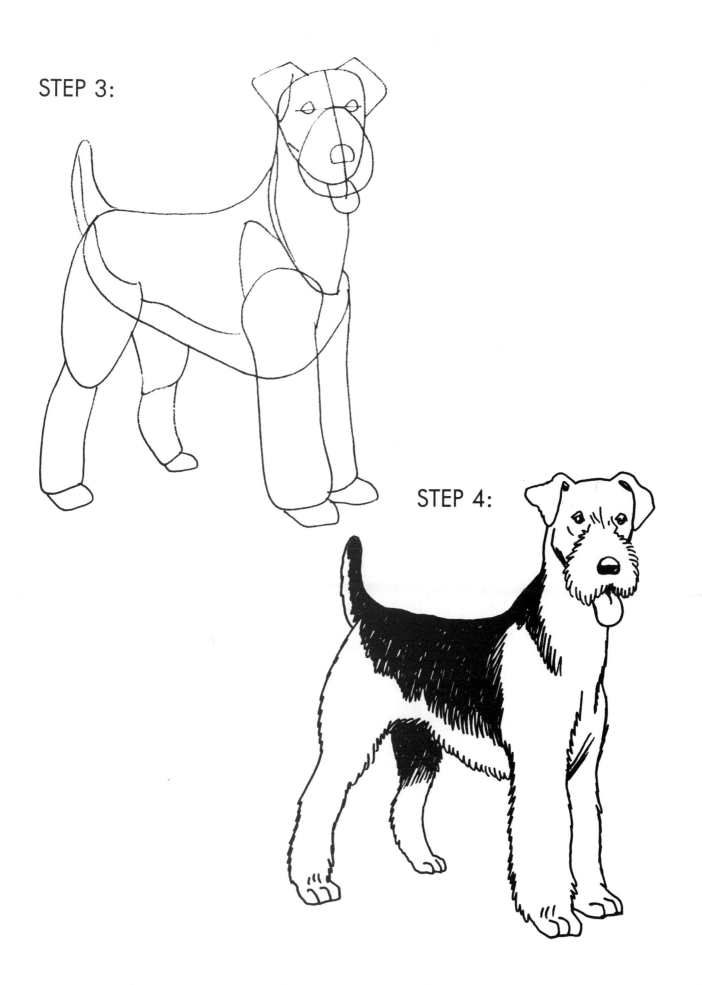

STEP 3:

STEP 4:

ENGLISH SETTER

STEP 1:

STEP 2:

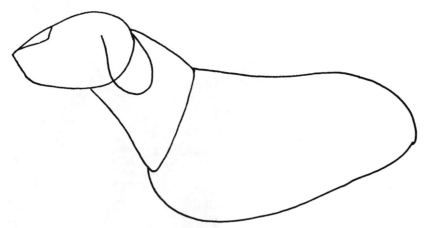

STEP 3:

STEP 4:

IRISH SETTER

STEP 1:

STEP 2:

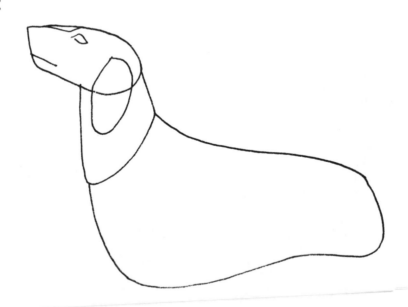

STEP 3:

STEP 4:

BOXER

STEP 1:

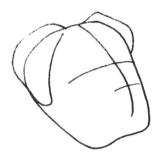

STEP 2:

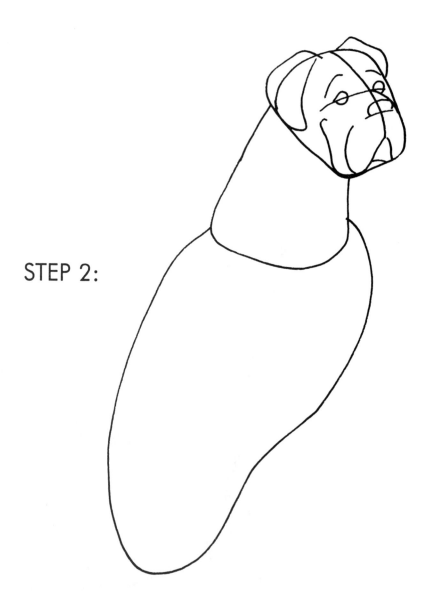

STEP 3:

STEP 4:

COCKER SPANIEL

STEP 1:

STEP 2:

STEP 3:

STEP 4:

BLOOD HOUND

STEP 1:

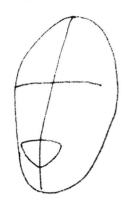

STEP 2:

STEP 3:

STEP 4:

BULLDOG

STEP 1:

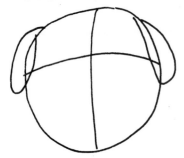

STEP 2:

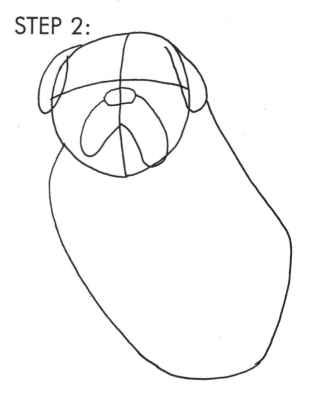

STEP 3:

STEP 4: